D1269675

So Audrey

CINDY DE LA HOZ

RUNNING PRESS

PHILADELPHIA · LONDON

A Running Press® Miniature Edition™
© 2016 by Cindy De La Hoz

Adapted from *So Audrey: 59 Ways to Put a Little Hepburn
in Your Step*, published in 2011 by Running Press,
a Member of the Perseus Books Group.

9 8 7 6 5 4 3 2 1
Digit on the right indicates the number of this printing

Library of Congress Control Number: 2015956779

ISBN 978-0-7624-6048-9

Running Press Book Publishers
A Member of the Perseus Books Group
2300 Chestnut Street
Philadelphia, PA 19103-4371

Visit us on the web!
www.runningpress.com

INTRODUCTION

Audrey Hepburn excelled like no other as a humanitarian, actress, and the absolute epitome of style. The breadth of her charitable work, helping children all over the world through UNICEF, affected millions. In terms of acting, she won dozens of awards and left behind a legacy of films that still resonate with audiences today. As if that weren't enough, this remarkable woman also taught us how to achieve style in a manner that's posh, polished, and comfortable, to boot. The name "Audrey" has even become a byword for expressing admiration for simple good fashion sense. Women who emulate her style, consciously or not, can hope for the thrill of being told on any given day that their look is "so Audrey!"

While we now consider Audrey Hepburn's look undeniably timeless, it was considered daring in her youth. To appreciate the full import of the lessons she taught the world about fashion, one must remember that Audrey reached the United States from Europe in the early 1950s, an era when Marilyn Monroe was on the rise and popularizing a shapely hourglass figure with her sexy sense of style. Audrey's was the polar opposite of that look.

No one had seen anything like this European export! Her face was certainly one of a kind. One of Audrey's iconic movies, *Funny Face*, is a tribute to her "quirky" features; the separate parts—huge doe-like eyes, a prominent nose, full brows, slightly off-kilter teeth—all happened to add up to a perfectly charming face. Hollywood accepted that, but confronted with her gamine figure, the natural inclination for studio designers of the day was to help this girl out—pad the hips, pad the bra, cinch the waist to highlight what curves she did have. What they didn't count on was Audrey's polite but firm resistance to the fashion makeover they had in mind.

Audrey may have been small, but she was no pushover. She had taste and innate fashion sense cultivated during her upbringing in Europe. Most importantly, she knew instinctively what looked good on her, and she wasn't about to let anyone make her look silly. At 5'7", Audrey didn't feel the urge to add length to her frame with high heels, so she wore flats, or kitten heels, at best. She preferred slim lines to padded clothes, so she wore fitted tops, crisp button-down shirts, and cropped slacks, often in black.

Feeling pressure to conform from Hollywood stylists, Audrey turned to a then fledgling fashion designer in Paris, Hubert de Givenchy. Together, Hepburn and Givenchy revolutionized the world of fashion through their collaborations on her personal wardrobe and on many of her most famous films. The classic *Breakfast at Tiffany's* alone blessed us with the Little Black Dress and helped popularize kitten heels, streaked highlights, oversized sunglasses, trench coats, the statement necklace—and yes, eating fruit Danish in the most posh setting possible.

Look at any photo of Audrey or watch her in *Sabrina*, *Charade*, *Funny Face*, *Two for the Road*, or *How to Steal a Million*, and you'll see why she became a fashion icon in her own time and for generations to come. She never thought the attention was warranted, though. In Audrey's words, "Truly, I've never been concerned with any public image. It would drive me around the bend if I worried about the pedestal others have put me on. And also I don't believe it." Audrey's looks, talent, and good works are not all that make her a fabulous role model for women of all ages. She also had heart and humility—both wildly attractive traits in a beautiful woman.

This book was inspired by an appreciation for everything about Audrey Hepburn that makes her a stellar person to look up to, but as an ode to the lady who gave us more timeless wardrobe pieces than any stylish star, the focus here will be on fashion. What follows are fifty-nine easy ways that you can put a little Hepburn in your step, and earn that most coveted of fashion compliments, "That's so Audrey!"

YOU CAN NEVER GO
WRONG WITH A
little black

THE ONLY
competition
for the little
black dress—

the little

white dress.

MIX IT UP WITH A
splash of color
TO BRIGHTEN
YOUR DAY.

HEELS

can bring you pain,

but a

ballet flat

will never hurt you.

Skip the flip-flops in the summer —opt for strappy GLADIATOR SANDALS.

Sunglasses

... THE LARGER
THE BETTER.

A GLORIOUS SUN HAT

offers class—
and prevents unsightly
squinting.

Sometimes

CLASSIC
menswear

looks better on ladies.

Never
underestimate
the
importance
of
beauty rest.

COMPASSION

*—it wears very
well indeed.*

When a late-summer chill hits the air, ALWAYS HAVE A CARDIGAN ON HAND.

Nothing lends
an air of mystery
better than a

CLASSIC
TRENCH
COAT.

Don't question "seasonal pants"

—the effortless style of

white
slacks

is always in fashion.

A stylish

HEADSCARF

will always

make you

stand out in

a crowd.

Eyeliner
and
mascara
—the ultimate
DYNAMIC DUO.

A TOUCH OF
ULTRA-GLAMOROUS
ANIMAL
PRINT
GOES A LONG WAY.

For an unexpected twist, try a *plunging back* instead of neckline.

FOR AUDREY IT WAS GIVENCHY PERFUME —NOTHING LINGERS IN THE MEMORY MORE POTENTLY THAN A *signature fragrance.*

NEATLY SHAPED

full brows

DRAW ATTENTION
TO THE EYES.

Get into the
BOHEMIAN SPIRIT
and find your ideal

HOOP
earrings.

Whether it be a mission of peace or pleasure, SOAK UP THE LOCAL COLOR along your travels.

Side swept,
choppy, or straight—
there is a

perfect
fringe

for all face shapes.

Don't take
fashion
too seriously...
let your
sense of humor
shine through.

A one-shoulder dress

equals instant

HIGH FASHION.

Nothing
illuminates
quite like that

*motherly
glow.*

Who says you can't wear horizontal stripes?

Love the "funny

IT'S THE ONLY

face" in the mirror—
ONE YOU HAVE.

For an angelic appearance—

HEAD-TO-TOE

WHITE.

For
the
essence
of the
Left Bank—

head-to-

toe black.

Even a
paper cup
becomes
elegant
when
clutched
by an

opera
glove.

A SMILE
is your best accessory—
use it to spread joy.

Audrey had a fawn named Ip. Nurture your love of animals— and inspire adorable photo ops—with an *unconventional* PET.

TONED

ARMS

—always worth a standing ovation.

Let a

STATEMENT
NECKLACE

do the talking.

Whether torn for effect,
stone-washed, or dyed indigo,
NOTHING BEATS
A GREAT PAIR OF
blue jeans.

A TRUSTED HAIRSTYLIST

is worth their weight in gold

To pull off any look,

WEAR IT WITH
CONFIDENCE.

The

ALL-PURPOSE
SCARF

tied around the neck,
to a belt loop,
or around the head,

gives a dash of flair.

DRAMATIC EYES
and
nude lips
—a brilliant balancing act.

Regular exercise is more fun—and infinitely cuter— *with a friend.*

A BOAT-NECK CUT ACCENTUATES

an elegant collarbone and neck

STOCK UP
ON CROPPED PANTS IN
COLORS
AND
PATTERNS.

A "mod" fashion staple in the '60s and stylish in any era—every woman needs a pair of

KNEE-HIGH
BOOTS.

PATENT LEATHER

—be it shoes or an entire suit—

always inspires envy.

Don't shy away from

UNUSUAL
ACCESSORIES

—make a statement!

Achieve the pinnacle of panache—study

BREAKFAST AT TIFFANY'S.

A dose of humility makes a beautiful woman IRRESISTIBLE.

SHOULDERS BACK!

Any ensemble can
benefit from

good posture.

Highlights

are a

STREAK OF

GENIUS.

Don't be shy—
there is a shade of
red lipstick
for every woman.

Treat yourself—an *investment handbag* IS MADE TO LAST.

A DENIM JACKET

is that essential piece

TO GIVE A LADY
AN EDGE.

A HEALTHY DIET

IS VITAL, BUT WHEN IT'S

YOUR BIRTHDAY—

*have your cake
and eat it, too!*

POP DOWN THE BRIM
AND WEAR A
FEDORA
LIKE YOU MEAN IT.

Go preppy and playful

with a cute pair of

SAILOR SHORTS.

When spring arrives,
CELEBRATE WITH A
floral sun dress!

Floral arrangements
ARE CLEARLY **NOT** JUST FOR WEDDINGS.

Make a grand entrance and

DAZZLE

THE CROWD IN A

strapless evening gown.

YOU

HAVE A SENSE OF STYLE—

pass it on.

PHOTO CREDITS